P

BLESS THE DAUGHTER
RAISED BY A VOICE
IN HER HEAD

"With her first full-length poetry collection, Warsan Shire electrifies. Her poems capture young Black womanhood, what it means to search for home in the world, what it means to inhabit a woman's body, the tensions of reconciling faith and family and everything that threatens the borders of expectation and obligation. The beautifully crafted poems in this collection are fiercely tender gifts."

—Roxane Gay, author of *Bad Feminist* and *Hunger*

"Warsan Shire is both 'poet's poet' and 'poet of the people' the way Pablo Neruda and Gwendolyn Brooks were both poets beloved by poets as well as the people. *Bless the Daughter Raised by a Voice in Her Head* is full of ferocious love and truth. It is not overstatement to say Shire writes the way that Nina Simone sang. All the brilliance of her lean, monumental *Teaching My Mother How to Give Birth* is magnified in this remarkable new book."

—Terrance Hayes, author of *American Sonnets for My Past and Future Assassin*

"I have long been a massive fan of Warsan Shire's extraordinarily gifted poetry. Her exquisite, memorable, and finely tuned poems articulate a depth of experience that never fails to surprise and profoundly move me, as she so powerfully gives voice to the unspoken. This is a book of many gems, to be savored slowly, allowing each wonderful poem to sink in before progressing to the next one. I will certainly be returning to it again and again."

—Bernardine Evaristo, author of *Girl, Woman, Other*

"Warsan Shire's fierce and compelling book of poems should come with a warning label: *These poems will break your heart.* Never has the phrase 'Speak truth to power' been truer. But Shire does more than *speak* truth; she *sings* truth and that is precisely her power. Her poems are incantations, chants, spells for our time and all time. They address the displacements and violence experienced by migrants, refugees, those in dark bodies and in female bodies. Where else to go for safety and salve but poetry? Souls so deep that no cruelty or injustice can drown their song. A warrior woman poet, Shire wields words as weapons of mass creation. It is a 'war' every reader will want to fight with her. And we do, by reading and rereading her poems."

—Julia Alvarez, author of *In the Time of the Butterflies* and *Afterlife*

"Read these candid and revelatory poems to wrap your arms tight around the certainty of your own fracture, to acknowledge the many places and many ways your body has succumbed to violation and only fitfully healed. Read them to know your whole muscled self as a vessel for grief, and to bask in the stuttered lyric of its story. Beauty is maddeningly elusive, but it does exist. It's here in these lines, bursting brilliant, reshaping the story."

—Patricia Smith, author of *Incendiary Art*

"Heartbreaking, full-bodied, and luscious . . . If someone from another planet wanted to know what it was like for a woman to survive on earth, they should read this book."

—Pascale Petit, author of *Tiger Girl*

"Warsan Shire is an expert sculptor. She molds words into clay, her poems into statues—each one a wonder that I return to, in reverence. Because in every line, every curve is an invitation to see differently what has been deemed ugly or difficult. This book is the art gallery I've yearned to visit."

—Vivek Shraya, author of *I'm Afraid of Men* and *even this page is white*

"It is absolutely astonishing how much emotion, intelligence, imagination, and truth Warsan Shire can get into one collection. She is a poet of the highest order, with a compassionate heart and a limitless mind."

—Benjamin Zephaniah, author of *The Life and Rhymes of Benjamin Zephaniah*

BY WARSAN SHIRE

Teaching My Mother How to Give Birth
Her Blue Body

BLESS THE DAUGHTER
RAISED BY A VOICE
IN HER HEAD

BLESS THE DAUGHTER RAISED BY A VOICE IN HER HEAD

POEMS

Warsan Shire

RANDOM HOUSE

NEW YORK

A Random House Trade Paperback Original

Copyright © 2022 by Warsan Shire

Published in the United States by Random House, an imprint and division of
Penguin Random House LLC, New York.

RANDOM HOUSE and the HOUSE colophon are registered trademarks of Penguin
Random House LLC.

Published in the United Kingdom by Chatto & Windus, an imprint of Vintage, part
of Penguin Random House UK.

The following poems have been previously published, sometimes in different form:
from *Teaching My Mother How to Give Birth* (the mouthmark series, 2011): "Bless
Your Ugly Daughter" (modified from "Ugly"), "The Abubakr Girls Are Different"
(modified from "Things We Had Lost in the Summer"—*Teaching My Mother*, and
"Mermaids"—*Her Blue Body*), "Bless the Sharmuto" (modified from "Beauty"),
"Bless the Blood" (modified from "Birds"), and "To Swim with God" (modified
from "Trying to Swim with God"); featured in Beyoncé's *Lemonade:* "Unbearable
Weight of Staying," "Bless the Moon," and "Nail Technician as Palm Reader";
from *Her Blue Body* (the flap series, 2015, flipped eye publishing): "Midnight in the
Foreign Food Aisle," "Backwards," "Bless This House—The House," "Her Blue
Body Full of Light," "Bless Our Blue Bodies—Our Blue Bodies," and "Grief Has
Its Blue Hands in My Hair—Grief Has Its Blue Hands in Her Hair."

Library of Congress Cataloging-in-Publication Data
Names: Shire, Warsan, author.
Title: Bless the daughter raised by a voice in her head : poems / by Warsan Shire.
Description: New York : Random House, [2021]
Identifiers: LCCN 2020049178 (print) | LCCN 2020049179 (ebook) | ISBN
    9780593134351 (trade paperback) | ISBN 9780593134368 (ebook)
Subjects: LCGFT: Poetry.
Classification: LCC PR6119.H518 B55 2021 (print) | LCC PR6119.H518 (ebook) |
    DDC 821/.92—dc23
LC record available at https://lccn.loc.gov/2020049178
LC ebook record available at https://lccn.loc.gov/2020049179

PRINTED IN THE UNITED STATES OF AMERICA ON ACID-FREE PAPER

randomhousebooks.com

3rd Printing

FOR SAMAWADO, SUBAN AND SALMA

I was an ugly child
You were an ugly child
We were ugly children.

      —Hiromi Itō

Hooyo ma joogto, kabaheeda qaadatay.

Your mother isn't home, she left the house and took her shoes.

      —Somali children's lullaby

CONTENTS

ARE YOU THERE, GOD?

TESTAMENT

BLESS THE DAUGHTER RAISED BY A VOICE IN HER HEAD

WHAT DOESN'T KILL YOU

EXTREME GIRLHOOD

A loop, a girl born
to each family,
prelude to suffering.

Bless the baby girl,
caul of dissatisfaction,
patron saint of not
good enough.

Are you there, God?
It's me, Warsan.
Maladaptive daydreaming,
obsessive, dissociative.

Born to a lullaby
lamenting melanin,
newborn ears checked
for the first signs of color.

At first I was afraid, I was petrified.

The child reads surahs each night
to veil her from il
protecting body and home
from intruders.

She wakes with a fright,
someone cutting the rope,

something creeping
deep inside her.

Are you there, God?
It's me, the ugly one.

Bless the Type 4 child,
scalp massaged with the milk
of cruelty, cranium cursed,
crushed between adult knees,
drenched in pink lotion.

Everything you did to me,
I remember.

Mama, I made it
out of your home
alive, raised by
the voices
in my head.

ASSIMILATION

We never unpacked,
dreaming in the wrong language,
carrying our mother's fears in our feet—
  if he raises his voice we will flee
  if he looks bored we will pack our bags
unable to excise the refugee from our hearts,
unable to sleep through the night.

The refugee's heart has six chambers.
In the first is your mother's unpacked suitcase.
In the second, your father cries into his hands.
The third room is an immigration office,
your severed legs in the fourth,
in the fifth a uterus—yours?
The sixth opens with the right papers.

I can't get the refugee out of my body,
I bolt my body whenever I get the chance.
How many pills does it take to fall asleep?
How many to meet the dead?

The refugee's heart often grows
an outer layer. An assimilation.
It cocoons the organ. Those unable to grow the extra skin
die within the first six months in a host country.

At each and every checkpoint the refugee is asked

are you human?

The refugee is sure it's still human but worries that overnight,
while it slept, there may have been a change in classification.

MY LONELINESS IS KILLING ME

He smokes until he sees something
moving in the smoke, remembers
joy like blindness: swimming at Jazeera
Beach, gorging on belonging, barwaaqo,

iftiin. He remembers riding through Suuqa Bakaaraha
on a motorbike, held onto by women with hair
trailing behind them like black smoke.

It's raining in London again, Hassan
Aden Samatar sings from a small, sullen
cassette player in the corner of the room,
tonight no one knows you.

Cidlada ka atkow, Abti—*be stronger than your loneliness*
Uncle, steam rises from qaxwo bitter with tears, carefully
rolling tobacco the same color as his hands.
He sings along. Alone this time, alone every time.

HOME

I

No one leaves home unless home is the mouth of a shark. You only run for the border when you see the whole city running as well. The boy you went to school with, who kissed you dizzy behind the old tin factory, is holding a gun bigger than his body. You only leave home when home won't let you stay.

No one would leave home unless home chased you. It's not something you ever thought about doing, so when you did, you carried the anthem under your breath, waiting until the airport toilet to tear up the passport and swallow, each mournful mouthful making it clear you would not be going back.

No one puts their children in a boat, unless the water is safer than the land. No one would choose days and nights in the stomach of a truck, unless the miles traveled meant something more than journey.

No one would choose to crawl under fences, beaten until your shadow leaves, raped, forced off the boat because you are darker, drowned, sold, starved, shot at the border like a sick animal, pitied. No one would choose to make a refugee camp home for a year or two or ten, stripped and searched, finding prison everywhere. And if you were to survive, greeted on the other side—*Go home Blacks, dirty refugees, sucking our country dry of milk, dark with their hands out, smell strange, savage, look what they've done to their own countries, what will they do to ours?*

The insults are easier to swallow than finding your child's body in the rubble.

I want to go home, but home is the mouth of a shark. Home is the barrel of a gun. No one would leave home unless home chased you to the shore. No one would leave home until home is a voice in your ear saying—*leave, run, now. I don't know what I've become.*

II

I don't know where I'm going. Where I came from is disappearing. I am unwelcome. My beauty is not beauty here. My body is burning with the shame of not belonging, my body is longing. I am the sin of memory and the absence of memory. I watch the news and my mouth becomes a sink full of blood. The lines, forms, people at the desks, calling cards, immigration officers, the looks on the street, the cold settling deep into my bones, the English classes at night, the distance I am from home. Alhamdulillah, all of this is better than the scent of a woman completely on fire, a truckload of men who look like my father—pulling out my teeth and nails. All these men between my legs, a gun, a promise, a lie, his name, his flag, his language, his manhood in my mouth.

BLESS MAYMUUN'S MIND

Maymuun only just began her prescription of sertraline 6 weeks ago, 50 mg daily to be upped to 100 mg if she still can't live like this. Maymuun smells jasmine suddenly and then nothing. Maymuun dreams of things to come. Maymuun spits and steam rises from that spit. The doctor won't know about the voices or her hands raw from washing. She imagines she will die here, alone, far from home. Maymuun calls family every month; salaams and confirmation of money order. Calling cards with images of leopards running through the Serengeti. A lone baobab tree, a single resting lion. The phone warms the side of her face like the sun. She listens to the clamoring voices, oh how blessed she is, how proud they are, how all their hopes depend on her, how walahi, all their dreams lie at her feet.

DAHABSHIIL SENDS BLESSINGS

She calls the dead, long-distance,
from a booth inside an Internet café,
coin-sized burns on both her wrists,
unable to imagine a life unbound
from statelessness or a soul untethered
from the Home Office. Indignity sits
slack-jawed with an indefinite leave
to remain, awaiting papers far into
the afterlife. Still, she promises
to send money.

BLESS THE BULIMIC

Insolent youth, spent
on my knees, sleep deprived,
sick, forgive me my prayers
to the God of thin women,
Istagfirullah, Ya Allah of jutting
ribs, forgive me please,
famine back home.

BLESS THE GHOST

My mother transported it
on her skin, shroud
circling her skull, matter
under her nails.

Her gynecologist thought
he saw something
between speculum and
cervix.

While she reads, it laps at her feet
like fire, she feels it sleeping
between them.

In the shower, it lathers her back
sometimes embracing her
from behind, weighing
her down.

She never meets its gaze,
thankful it keeps her warm.

II

Odor of unknown origin,
she washes her hair, smoke
of unseen fire—memory smuggled
deep inside dreams lush with grief,
stowed in her blood—an unrung bell,
an uncalled prayer, bless this child
born on sorrow's palm.

She recalls a time they worshipped
birds, kingdom of myrrh, damp
hands working her breast for lumps,
steam marbling her reflection.

To call her is to hear its wet breath
in the back, keeping track of the dead
children of Somalia, culled by war
and the white gloved hand of Europe.

She unfolds a small silk scarf,
to catch a tear, were it to fall
as dictators fall.

DROWNING IN DAWSON'S CREEK

Lately, the dreams have been different.
Something chasing me naked and blood-footed
through the woodland, something with strong arms
holding my head under cold creek water.

When the fishermen discover my carcass, the coroner
examining my corpse (bleached from submersion)
identifies my cadaver as Caucasian.

When I was twelve or thirteen and mad
with loneliness, I dreamt of white boys and
ladders leading to bedroom windows.
I dreamt all night of their scurrying, climbing
in and out of me.

For Pacey Witter I would hitchhike Capeside.
For his plaid embrace,
I was willing to disown myself.

The remains of a murdered Somali woman were found in Lewis County, Washington State, in 2010, and for a decade, her body was misidentified as Caucasian Jane Doe.

BLESS THE QUMAYO

who upon hearing news of a girl
child, lit torches of contempt to welcome
us onto this planet, stalking us
through our mothers' birth canals,
ululating, born on the month of isku
xishood—*have some shame*—the goat
slit from ear to ear. God help those
who gossip on the phone after Maghrib,
tallying the sluts of the family, the
sainted sharmuto, guessing
whose hymen fizzes after dark,
pink fading to black, what shadow
cast from our flag of dishonor,
verily your life is brimming
with sorrow, we've witnessed
love slowly abandon you, still,
we pray you find healing, bitch.

LULLABY FOR FATHER

Soo bari, aabo, inside your dream
nests a devoted woman singing
a song you once heard, the words of which you

almost recall before she is beheaded.
Your children are distant galaxies emitting
light that keeps you up. Rest your body, aabo,
heavy with distention, dreams lost in translation,

dreams of drifting in space, the rings of Saturn
around the neck of Layla, dreams macerated
under grief's gaze. Bless your drowsy blue slumber,
swayed by the patron saint of restlessness,

distilled in darkness, buoyed into sleep,
you hang on the edge of the moon, brown hands
dissolving like demerara, teeth loosen and float
out of your mouth like small bodies.

FILIAL CANNIBALISM

From time to time
mothers in the wild
devour their young,
an appetite born of
pure, bright need.
Occasionally,
mothers from ordinary
homes, much like our
own, feed on the viscid
shame their daughters
are forced to secrete
from glands formed
in the favor of men.

BLESS YOUR UGLY DAUGHTER

She knows loss intimately.
A child relatives avoided,
felt like splintered wood, smelt
of sea water, she reminded them
of thirst, of war.

As an infant forced to gargle rosewater,
smoked in uunsi to purify her of whatever
unclean thing she inherited.

Your daughter is covered in it.
Her teeth are small colonies,
her stomach is an island,
her thighs are borders.

So few will want to lay down
and watch the world burn
from their bedroom.

Your daughter's face is a small riot,
her hands are a civil war,
she has a refugee camp tucked
behind each ear, her body is a body littered
with ugly things

but God,
doesn't she wear
the world well.

THIS IS NOT A LOVE SONG

MIDNIGHT IN THE FOREIGN FOOD AISLE

Dear Uncle, is everything you love foreign
or are you foreign to everything you love?
We're all animals and the body wants what
it wants, trust me, I know. The blonde said
Come in, love, take off your coat, what do
you want to drink?

Love is not haram but after years of fucking
women who are unable to pronounce your name,
you find yourself totally alone, in the foreign
food aisle, beside the turmeric and saffron,
remembering your mother's warm, dark hands,
prostrating in front of the halal meat, praying in a
language you haven't used in years.

ARE YOU AFRAID OF THE DARK?

My mother is an olm
born without eyes
thriving in the dark
rare and translucent
sustained by so little.

PHOTOGRAPHS OF HOOYO
(HARLESDEN, 1990–2000)

1990

Hooyo exiting her
bedroom, tears in
her eyes, sorrow in her
colostrum, her real name
hiding from the government
in the plumes of uunsi smoke
behind her.

1993

Hooyo in the kitchen,
head bent in front of
her own personal Kaaba,
feverishly repeating *ameen*
in every pause, playing cassettes
sent from back home, ayeeyo's
grainy voice reciting duaa.

1994

Hooyo in the living room,
wearing a banana print diraac
singing her own raspy rendition
of Tracy Chapman's "Mountains

O' Things"—*justadi obadi one time.*
Olive oil in her Bantu knots, henna
drying on her hands.

1998

Hooyo standing under the apple
tree in my aunt's garden, her hair
cut short, wearing a cream trouser
suit and six small hoops in each ear,
she is looking up at the sky, overlined
lips slightly open.

2000

Hooyo in bed, holding negatives up
to the light, squinting at undeveloped ghosts,
names of the dead thrown behind her
like salt, her atrophied youth in storage,
mumbling Magool under her breath,
war flaying Somalia alive.

BLESS THE CAMELS

Bless those rare visits with father
in that halfway home shared with bereft men,
faint with the sweet, unsaintly scent of mildew.

At night, the Lord's lonely moon sliced through the room
illuminating our small faces, held captive to spinning stories,
his voice almost sonar, crackling deep in our chests.

We slept peacefully, after blessing the village he was born in,
the camels he slept beside, the deserts he wandered,
the stars he laid beneath, the hyenas' laughter in the wind,
son of a nomad, we slept peacefully after blessing him.

GLITTER ON THE MOUTH OF BOYS

The girls watch from beyond the glass as the boys ride BMX bikes like God
flicked them with God's middle finger. Front wheel in the air, a salute.

Rage ferments like camel milk, rage appears like mist. The girls hang
their torsos out of windows, watching boys skinning gold teeth, gleaming

24kt. Bless the glitter on the mouth of boys. Bless their dilated eyes.
Bless their topless bodies, smelling like outside. Bless

the soft interior of boys, velvet darkness expanding,
fading into smoke.

UNBEARABLE WEIGHT OF STAYING

I don't know when love became elusive.
My mother's laughter in a dark room.

What I know is that no one I knew had it.
My father's arms around my mother's neck.

A door halfway open.
Fruit too ripe to eat.

ABSOLUTELY FABULOUS

Chain-smoking under ill-formed
halos. Dark areolas blinking under
leopard print diraac. Car crash
of a life; a car outside with the engine
running.

Memories reach out of walls
dragging her by the hair. Baati
caught on door handles, pulling
her through time. At night her silk scarf
slips around her neck like a noose.

Bless her companions, their unhinged dreams
of luxury. Gazelles teetering in heels, careening
into mania. Diets of excess, deep allegiance
to the adage *"If you don't laugh, you'll cry."*
And they laugh so hard they weep.

HOOYO FULL OF GRACE

Paradise lies under the feet of your mother.

—Prophet Mohammed (Peace be upon him)

Goddess of absence, Holy Mother,
   Our Lady of Leaving Children
With Strangers, patron saint of

the babies will raise themselves.
   Our distant orb, our cold womb.
Breastmilk of our discontent.

Infants swaddled in blood, the bees
   bring messages of postpartum grief.
Your girlhood an incubation for madness.

Under your feet, the trapdoor to heaven
   opens its mouth, its teeth
grazing your toes.

MY FATHER, THE ASTRONAUT

If the moon was Europe, my father was an astronaut who died on his
    way to the moon.
My father, the failed moonwalker, blinded by space. My father, the
    Black cosmonaut, frenzied
by thirst. My father who heard the voice of God, clear as the call to
    prayer, suspended in that dark desert.
My father who wore a spacesuit slashed by longing, spinning towards
    the vast desolate.
On a night when the angels have drawn back their wings, you may
    glimpse my father
hurtling through space, his body carried by gravity's absence, blood
    collecting in his head,
his tears pink, gelatinous clots, unable to fall.

SAINT HOOYO

Hooyo with a beauty mark
above her lip, qibla,
Hooyo dyes her hair in the sink.
Hooyo knows someone's been watching
porn on the family computer.
Hooyo doesn't call your bluff.
Hooyo saw you climb out of that man's car last night.
Hooyo found your stash.
Hooyo sees you sinking, swimming with the orcas.
Hooyo prays for your salvation.
Hooyo understands your stump of a tongue.
Hooyo saw the blood.

Hooyo, patron saint of
   my children have different passports to me.
Hooyo, blessed saint of
   raising them too far from home.

   I don't recognize my own children
     they speak and dream in the wrong language
      as much as I understand
       it may as well be the language of birds.

BLESS OUR CCTV STAR

Ma'am / is that your brother /
being breastfed / by hooded
goons / are those your brother's
teeth / caught on speed cameras /
eroding in real time / is that your
brother's face / marred by pixelation /
you say you're able to recognize
him / from any distance / and from this distance
you say the figures appeared to be /
swaying / under the moon's cordial light? /
And you say one of those dark
figures / may have been Azrael /
with his scythe tucked / under his
chin / like a violin / and the notes
he played / you say you already
heard in a dream?

In Islam, Azrael is the angel of death who separates souls from their bodies.

JOYRIDE

In your sleeping mother's car,
warm as cattle, you and your mates
huddle in ill light, to her heartbreak.

Bless the mandem, stunted children
squinting, overexposed, silver
teeth catching each glint, smoke

weeping from dark, perfect lips.
Your tired mother turns in her veneer
of sleep, dreaming in the scent of jasmine.

Speed cameras track your escape from tunnels
of youth. An animal standing on hind legs
pretending to understand why it must die.

The flashlight taps the window.

BACKWARDS

The poem can start with him walking backwards into a room.
He takes off his jacket and sits down for the rest of his life,
that's how we bring Dad back.
I can make the blood run back up my nose, ants rushing into a hole.
We grow into smaller bodies, my breasts disappear,
your cheeks soften, teeth sink back into gums.
I can make us loved, just say the word.
Give them stumps for hands if even once they touched us without consent,
I can write the poem and make it disappear.
Step-dad spits liquor back into glass,
Mum's body rolls back up the stairs, the bone pops back into place,
maybe she keeps the baby.
Maybe we're okay, kid?
I'll rewrite this whole life and this time there'll be so much love,
you won't be able to see beyond it.

You won't be able to see beyond it,
I'll rewrite this whole life and this time there'll be so much love.
Maybe we're okay, kid,
maybe she keeps the baby.
Mum's body rolls back up the stairs, the bone pops back into place,
Step-dad spits liquor back into glass.
I can write the poem and make it disappear,
give them stumps for hands if even once they touched us without consent,
I can make us loved, just say the word.

Your cheeks soften, teeth sink back into gums
we grow into smaller bodies, my breasts disappear.
I can make the blood run back up my nose, ants rushing into a hole,
that's how we bring Dad back.
He takes off his jacket and sits down for the rest of his life.
The poem can start with him walking backwards into a room.

BLESS THE REAL HOUSEWIFE

Blessed be those who sit and wait
so hooyo sits, waiting for him to die.

Calcifying her one human body, staying
for the sake of the kids, then staying
for the sake of staying, enduring,
abstaining, waiting for the angel of death.

She explains how much harder it is to leave
the second marriage, that she doesn't want to
raise children the way she had to raise us,
and *What would people say?*

I ask *What if you die while you're waiting?*

In a recurring dream,
the one where she's driving alone at dawn
along a dirt road, passing by grazing camels,
her braid coming loose in the breeze, the sun
lifting its skirt, a peaceful Somalia in her rearview.
She thinks of this, and laughs.

ARE YOU THERE, GOD?

HOOYO ISN'T HOME .

AFTER IDRA NOVEY

When we were 5, 6 or 7.
When the war back home wouldn't end.
While our mothers were sleeping.
While our milk teeth were forced down our gullets.
Before Israfil puckered his lips and let out a breath.
Before areolas spread like ink.
Beyond the soft insides of dates.
Beyond the mirror, something watches.
After it crawled into your bedroom on its haunches.
After you tore out most of your hair.
As our mothers take us to exorcists.
As tentacles slide out from beneath our skirts.
While the statistics show 1 in 3 girls, 1 in 5 boys.
While the holy man douses us with tahlil.
When the body remembers, it bucks wildly.
When we try to heal, the phantom smell returns.
While in the shower, you break down.
While you wash your body you realize it is not your body.
And at the same time, it is the only body you have.

THE ABUBAKR GIRLS ARE DIFFERENT

The summer the Abubakr girls return home, we sit
    in a circle by the apple tree
        in their mother's garden.

All five of them seem older. Amel's hardened nipples push
    through the paisley of her blouse, minarets
        calling men to worship.

Daughter is synonymous with traitor,
    their father mutters
        in his sleep.

Before they left, we were the same, our bird chests clinking,
    long skirted-figurines waiting to grow
        into our hunger.

One of them pushes my open knees closed. *Sit like a girl.*
    I finger the hole in my shorts,
        shame warming my skin.

Juwariyah, my age, leans in and whispers
    I started my period.

Her hair is in my mouth when I try to move in closer,
    How did it feel?

After the procedure, the girls learn how to walk again, mermaids
     with new legs, soft knees buckling under
          their raw, sinless bodies.

We lie in bed beside each other, holding mirrors
     to the mouths of our skirts,
          comparing wounds.

BLESS THIS SCHOOL FOR GIRLS

Falis taught us more about our bodies
than we'd ever glean from the curriculum;
periods, uterus contractions, early symptoms
of cysts, signs of infertility, abortions and where
they were punishable by death, miscarriage—
how long it took to pass the clots and why
you shouldn't flush as a reflex. Our lady of red
rags—bless her—no one ever thought to ask
how or why she knew these things.

BLESS HOOYO'S KOHL-RIMMED EYES

We were obsessed, in orbit, gazing
as she ground galena into dust, rimming
her eyes with darkness, no reflective
surface necessary, Allah guiding her hand
steady as the dead. We spent our youth
watching her drag stibnite through pink
flesh of lacrimal papilla, our tearless wonder,
standing over uunsi with legs parted,
smoke at her ankles. At school we'd
mimic, pouting, lining our bright eyes with borrowed
4B pencils. The boys would see us and whisper *Witch*
to which our heads would tip, like synchronized
swimmers, cackling as our uvulas fluttered.

BLESS THE SHARMUTO

My sister soaps between her legs, her hair a prayer of curls.
It's 4 A.M. and she winks at me, bending over the sink,
small breasts bruised from sucking, gap-tooth smile,
popping her gum before saying—*don't forget,*

boys are haram.

Some nights we hear her in her room screaming.
The adults play Surah Al Baqarah to drown her out.
Anything that leaves her mouth sounds like sex,
our mother has banned her from saying God's name.

BLESS THE MOON

Forgive us, we blamed you
for floods, for the flush of blood,
for men who are also wolves, even
though you could pull the tide in
by her hair, we tell everyone
we walked all over you. We
blame you for the dark, as if you had
a choice, performing just beyond
the glass, distant and adored,
near but alone, cold and unimaginable
following us home. We use you
to see our blue bodies beneath
your damp light, we let you watch,
swollen against the glass as we move
against one another like fish.

THE BABY-SITTERS CLUB

To be baptized Tiffany,
Kimberly, a child dreaming
in the language of white suburbia,
praying at Clarissa's wide bay windows,
fading into another life, stitching
my body into the body of Home-
coming Queen, rising, stretching
my white body, in my white underwear,
sprawled on white sheets, the white light
of the sun shining through white linen
drapes, beyond which white clouds
are punctured by a white god
stretching his white arm from
out a white sky, while a white
limousine waits at my door.

TRICHOTILLOMANIA

We found something crouching behind your bed,
it grunted when approached, sang a severed song,
a dead thing clinging to life, a mass of knots,
born of fiber, torn from blood vessels, dry to the touch.

When it stood, it was the height of a shrill scream,
we asked its name, it said your name.

In the garden we set fire to it, it burnt quickly,
made a neonatal sound, left behind the perfume
of scorched sulfur. Was it yours?

BLESS THIS HOUSE

Mother says there are locked rooms inside all women.
Sometimes, the men—they come with keys,
and sometimes, the men—they come with hammers.

Nin soo joog laga waayo, soo jiifso aa laga helaa,
A man who won't listen to words, will listen to action.
I said *Stop,* I said *No* and he heard nothing.

Perhaps she has a plan, perhaps she takes him back to hers.
Perhaps he wakes up hours later in a bathtub full of ice,
dry mouth, flinching at his new, neat incision.

I point to my body and say *Oh, this old thing? No, I just slipped it on.*

Are you going to eat that? I say to my mother, pointing
to my father on the dining room table, mouth stuffed with a red apple.

The bigger my body is, the more locked rooms I find. The more men
    queue at the door. Ahmed didn't push it all the way in, I still think
    about what he could have opened up inside of me. Ali hesitated at
    the door for three years. Johnny with the blue eyes came with a bag
    of tools he'd used on other women: one hairpin, a bottle of bleach,

a switchblade and a jar of Vaseline. Yusuf called out God's name
through the keyhole and no one answered.
Some begged, some climbed up the side of my body like moss
looking for a way in. Some said they were on their way and never came.

Show us on the doll where you were touched, they said.
I said *I didn't look like a doll, I looked more like a house.*
They said *Show us on the house.*

Like this: two fingers down the drain.
Like this: a fist through the drywall.

My first found a trapdoor in my armpit, he fell in, hasn't been seen since.
Once in a while I feel a quickening, something small crawling up.
I might let him out. Maybe he's met the others—males
missing from cities or small towns and pleasant mothers,
who tricked and forced their way in.

Knock knock.
Who's there?
No one.

At parties I point to my body and say
Oh, this old thing? This is where men come to die.

ANGELA BASSETT BURNING IT ALL DOWN

That year, the wives in my family packed secret suitcases,
eyed the front door, fumbled with lighter fluid.

One stabbed her man in the groin, said
the look of disbelief in his eyes made it worth it.

Bitches' Hysteria the men called it.
Natural response the women named it.

Mother did not snap, instead she stretched, watching yeast ferment,
instead she busied herself with the process of preserving meat.

For years I've watched from the corner of my eye,
willing her to burn it all down.

In 1995, the film Waiting to Exhale *was released on VHS.*

BLESS THE BLOOD

Sofia used pigeon blood on her wedding night.
Next day, over the phone, she told me
her husband smiled when he saw the sheets,

how he gathered them under his nose,
closed his eyes and dragged his tongue over the stain.
She mimicked his baritone, how he whispered

her name—Sofia,
pure, chaste, untouched.
We giggled over the static.

After he praised her, she smiled, rubbed his head,
imagined his mother back home parading blood-
soaked sheets through the town,

waving at balconies, swollen with pride,
arms fleshy wings bound to her body,
ignorant of flight.

BURAANBUR

The woman in the center whirls until the whites of her eyes shine, spinning endlessly inside a swarm of women who all resemble her mother. Her silk garbasaar falls exposing tight black curls, her earrings snap away tearing through both lobules, her skin is covered in beads of sweat, glitter scattered across her face like ghost ants. The women form a tighter circle around her flailing body, clapping until something comes loose, comes undone, until something makes itself known. Her molars are paved in gold, kohl bleeding down her cheeks. The women clap until they see tufts emerge from her shoulder blades. The women chant *ii kacay, dhiigaa ii kacay, it's rising, the blood is rising*. Bless the catheter sting of womanhood. She begins to blur, almost breaking into light, her foot a beak hammering the ground, a thousand inkaar erased. Adorned in gold, my mother the child bride sits to the side, unsmiling, unbreathing.

TESTAMENT

TO SWIM WITH GOD

We're practicing back strokes at the local swimming pool
when I think of Kadija, how her body must've felt
as it fell from the twenty-fourth floor.

The instructor tells us the longest
a human being has held their breath underwater
is 22 minutes and 22 seconds. At home in the bath,
my hair swells to the surface, I stay submerged
until it burns, I think of everything I let slip through my fingers.

Inna lillahi Wa inna ilayhi Rajioon.

Hooyo says no one can fight it—
the body returning to God,
if it must, your body will leave without you.

To land face first, wearing a white cotton baati
hair untied and smoked with uunsi:
did Kadija believe she would float?

HER BLUE BODY FULL OF LIGHT

Can you believe I have cancer? Yosra asks,
a mug of tea between her hands,
almost laughing, hair cut close to her scalp.
I imagine the cancer auditioning
inside her body, tiny translucent slivers
of light weaving in and out of her abdomen
and uterus, traveling up and through her throat,
needle points of light, fireworks glimmering down, the body
burning into itself, deep sea blue inside
her body, her ribcage an aquarium,
the cancer spreading and spreading, deep space,
her throat a lava lamp, sparklers beneath breastbone—
a light show, a million tiny jellyfish, orchestral womb,
kaleidoscopic ovaries, disco ball heart,
her skin glowing and glowing,
lit from within.

BLESS OUR BLUE BODIES

I have dreamt of you suspended
in amniotic fluid, your hair fanned
out and alive, long again, before the cancer.
Undying, our movements synchronized,
us, tied together at the navel,
umbilical cord and all its length tugging
at me, far as it might extend. Gregory Porter climbing
through *there will be no love that's dying
here*—his voice, and how it soothes you from
beyond the distant wall of this maybe womb,
the faint rhythm of a larger heart
above.

EARTH TO YOSRA

Come in, can you hear
me? I still dream of you
every night since, in these
dreams I pick up the phone
to call you, Earth to Yosra.

Is death a gauzy dream,
can you see us?
Is it scientific, deep
space, deep sea? Are you
alright? Remember
when we'd eat chips
soaked in vinegar at pebble
beach, my fingers in your hair,
wrapping strands around
my index finger, over and
over, watching the water do
what only the water can.

Earth to Yosra,
Yosra to Earth.

VICTORIA IN ILLIYIN

Our Victoria growing gills in paradise, arms outstretched
in joy, wading in rivers of warm milk, swimming with the lost
babies of Eden, back strokes in the streams of heaven.
Our Victoria, gently carried out of the water on the shoulders
of angels, tenderly placed on the upturned palm of God.
Blessings to our sweet Victoria, rewarded with 72 devoted mothers
who delicately dry her small body with wool softer than skin.

Victoria Climbié (1991–2000) was an Ivorian child raised away from her parents by extended family. She was tortured and murdered by her great-aunt and great-aunt's boyfriend in a London flat. She died aged 8 with 128 injuries on her body.

GRIEF HAS ITS BLUE HANDS IN MY HAIR

She sleeps all day,
dreams of you in both worlds,
tills the blood in and out of her uterus,
wakes up smelling of zinc.

Grief sedated by orgasm,
orgasm heightened by grief.

God was in the room
when the man said to the woman
*I love you so much wrap your legs
around me pull me in pull me in pull
me in pullme in pull mein
pullmein.*

It smelt like flowers the last time she
buried the friend with the kind eyes.
The last time she buried her face
into his mattress, frangipani.

Her hips grind,
pestle and mortar,
cinnamon and cloves.
Whenever he pulls out:
loss.

BLESS THE GUN TOSSED INTO A RIVER

AFTER "FREEDOM OF LOVE" BY ANDRÉ BRETON

My brother with a fistfight for a mouth,
with teeth a row of innocent men waiting to die,
with fingers of lit spliffs sparking amber.

My brother with the throat of a gun tossed into a river,
and a bag of ice for a father, skin the color of a
Crimewatch reconstruction, a tongue of prolonged grief.

My brother with the heart of a knife dashed into the river,
with teeth capped like the life spans of his closest friends,
with the manic laughter of a fever dream.

                                              My brother

with eyes like gashes bleeding in the dark,
whose prison letters I memorized like surah,
like song.

BARWAAQO

Hooyo is young again
breath of sweet guava
oud-scented, turmeric
glow, soft as ripe mango,
reclining on rooftops of silk,
desert flowers tucked in her hair,
Killer singing softly about love and fate,
mist draped over her bare, brown knees,
a war-mottled future blown away into space.

BLESS GRACE JONES

Holy Mother of those deemed intimidating,
patron saint of the unapproachable,
savior of those told to soften their expression.

Our lady of uncomfortable silences,
Dame Grace Jones, your daughters
(damn their insomnia) turn in their dreamless sleep,
a legion of women flinching at touch.
Fortify them.

Monarch of the last word,
darling of the dark, arched brow,
we bless you, queen of the cut eye.

We lay our burdens at your feet,
careful not to weigh you down,
                from you, we are learning
to put ourselves first.

NAIL TECHNICIAN AS PALM READER

The nail technician pushes my cuticles
back, turns my hand over,
stretches the skin on my palm
and says, I see your daughters
and their daughters.

That night, in a dream, the first girl emerges
from a slit in my stomach. The scar heals
into a tight smile. The person I love pulls
the stitches out with their fingernails, black sutures
curling on the side of the bath.

I wake as the second girl crawls
head first up my throat—
a flower, blossoming
out of the hole in my face.

GLOSSARY

Aabo: Father.

Abti: Uncle.

Alhamdulillah: Glory be to God.

Ayeeyo: Grandmother.

Azrael: The angel of death.

Baati: Somali house dress.

Barwaaqo: Utopia.

Buraanbur: A traditional poetic form composed by Somali women, accompanied by dance and drumming, performed as a celebration.

Crimewatch: British television program that reconstructs major unsolved crimes in the UK.

Dahabshiil: Africa's largest money transfer company, Somali owned.

Diraac: Somali silk dress.

Duaa: Prayer to God.

Garbasaar: Somali silk shawl.

Haram: Forbidden.

Home Office: Department of government responsible for immigration.

Hooyo: Mother.

Iftiin: Bright light.

Il: Evil eye in Somali culture.

Illiyin: Supreme paradise, highest level of heaven.

Inkaar: A curse.

Inna lillahi Wa inna ilayhi Rajioon: To God we belong, to God we return.

Israfil: The angel who blows into the trumpet to signal the day of judgment.

Istagfirullah: God forgive me.

Jazeera Beach: Beautiful beach in Mogadishu.

Kaaba: Rests within the Great Mosque of Mecca, represents the metaphorical house of God.

Killer: Ahmed Shariif Killer, late Somali singer.

Maghrib: Dusk prayer.

Magool: The late Xalimo Khaliif Magool, Somali musician.

Olm: Cave salamander.

Oud: Fragrant incense.

Qaxwo: Spiced Somali coffee.

Qibla: The direction faced in prayer.

Qumayo: A cruel person.

Salaams: Islamic greetings.

Hassan Aden Samatar: Somali musician.

Sharmuto: Slut.

Small bodies: Meteoroids, asteroids, minor planets and comets found throughout the solar system.

Soo bari, aabo: Good night, Father.

Stibnite: Sulfide mineral used to make kohl.

Surah: Chapter of Quran.

Surah Al Baqarah: Surah from the Quran to ward off evil.

Suuqa Bakaaraha: Open market in Mogadishu.

Tahlil: Water blown into after reciting verses from Quran.

Trichotillomania: A disorder that involves recurrent, irresistible urge to pull out body hair.

Type 4: Hair type—tight perfectly coiled strands.

Uunsi: Somali incense.

Walahi: I swear to God.

ACKNOWLEDGMENTS

Eternal gratitude to Jacob Sam-La Rose, Nii Ayikwei Parkes, Samar Hammam, Clara Farmer, Caitlin McKenna, Parisa Ebrahimi, Deborah Sun de la Cruz, Bernardine Evaristo, Nathalie Teitler, Kwame Dawes, Patience Agbabi, Kadija George, Pascale Petit, Nick Makoha, Malika Booker, Paola Splendore, Naomi Woddis, Leyla Jeyte, Roger Robinson, Saharla Abdulkarim, Karen McCarthy Woolf, Terrance Hayes, Ladan Abdirahman, Martha Adams, Inua Ellams, Be Ogunsanya, Kayo Chingonyi, Sheila Ruiz, Teju Cole, Mukhtara Yusuf, Nahel Tzegai, Effi Ibok, Bahia Watson, Beyoncé Knowles-Carter, Yvette Noel-Schure, Kwasi Fordjour, Yosra El-Essawy and Yomi Sode.

Infinite love to my family and friends for their relentless support. To my husband, thank you for your love which has strengthened me. To my children, thank you for illuminating my world. My life is filled with joy because of you.

Warsan Shire is a Somali British writer and poet born in Nairobi and raised in London. She has written two chapbooks, *Teaching My Mother How to Give Birth* and *Her Blue Body*. She was awarded the inaugural Brunel International African Poetry Prize and served as the first Young Poet Laureate of London. She is the youngest member of the Royal Society of Literature and is included in the Penguin Modern Poets series. Shire wrote the poetry for the Peabody Award–winning visual album *Lemonade* and the Disney film *Black Is King* in collaboration with Beyoncé Knowles-Carter. She also wrote the short film *Brave Girl Rising*, highlighting the voices and faces of Somali girls in Africa's largest refugee camp.

Shire lives in Los Angeles with her husband and two children. *Bless the Daughter Raised by a Voice in Her Head* is her debut full-length poetry collection.

warsanshire.squarespace.com

Twitter: @warsan_shire

Instagram: @warsanshiree

ALL PRAISE DUE TO THE MOST HIGH.

ABOUT THE TYPE

This book was set in Bembo, a typeface based on an old-style Roman face that was used for Cardinal Pietro Bembo's tract *De Aetna* in 1495. Bembo was cut by Francesco Griffo (1450–1518) in the early sixteenth century for Italian Renaissance printer and publisher Aldus Manutius (1449–1515). The Lanston Monotype Company of Philadelphia brought the well-proportioned letterforms of Bembo to the United States in the 1930s.